CHATTAHOOCHEE

CHATTAHOOCHEE

POEMS BY

PATRICK PHILLIPS

The University of Arkansas Press

Fayetteville

2004

Copyright © 2004 by The University of Arkansas Press

All rights reserved
Manufactured in Korea by Pacifica Communications

08   07   06   05   04   5   4   3   2   1

Designed by Ellen Beeler

⊗ The paper used in this publication meets the minimum requirements
of the American National Standard for Permanence of Paper for Printed
Library Materials Z39.48-1984.

Library of Congress Cataloging-in-Publication Data

Phillips, Patrick, 1970–
   Chattahoochee : poems / by Patrick Phillips.
      p. cm.
   ISBN 1-55728-775-9 (pbk. : alk. paper)
   I. Title.
   PS3616.H465C48 2004
   811'.6—dc22

                                                      2004006373

FOR

SID & CAM

Acknowledgments

Grateful acknowledgment is made to the following publications in which these poems first appeared:

"The Doves," *Agni*; "The Mussel," *Black Warrior Review*; "The Chimney," *DoubleTake*; "Chattahoochee," *The Gettysburg Review*; "Elegy Ending in a Dream," "The Rules," "Pictures of the Dead," *Gulf Coast*; "My Lovely Assistant," *Meridian*; "In the Museum of Your Last Day," *The Nation*; "To the Muse, from Way Downtown," "My Father, Playing Tennis," "To Fortune," "Ars Videndi," *New England Review*; "Two Figures," *Nimrod*; "The Doe," *Poetry*; "Baptism," *Quarterly West*; "The Reptilian Ancestry of Birds," "My Brother on Lake Lanier," *Rivendell*; "Twelve Views of My Father," "Blue Ridge Bestiary," *Virginia Quarterly Review*.

"Elegy Ending in a Dream" was the poem of the day for December 21, 2002, on *Poetry Daily* (www.poems.com) and appeared as a collaboration with the artist Paul Corrigan on bornmagazine.com, February 2004.

"The Doves" is after "Duerne" by the Danish poet Paul la Cour, from his collection *Mellem Bark og Ved* (1950).

To my mother and father, my sister and brother, and especially to my wife Ellen—*love and endless thanks*. I am also deeply grateful to Claude Barbre, Chin Chong, Michael Collier, Deborah Digges, Steve Duffy, Ted Genoways, Jennifer Grotz, Mary Stewart Hammond, Gary Hawkins, Jeff Hayden, Kristin Henderson, A. Van Jordan, Sebastian Matthews, Michael McCann, Stanley Plumly, Martha Rhodes, Alan Shapiro, Enid Shomer, Tom Sleigh, Ellen Bryant Voigt, and C. Dale Young. And for their vital support, thanks to the MacDowell and Millay Colonies, the U.S. Fulbright Commission, the Unterberg Poetry Center, New York University, the University of Arkansas Press, and most importantly, the Bread Loaf Writers' Conference.

Contents

CHATTAHOOCHEE

THE DOVES

If I could call the doves
together in the field,
call with the voice
of open hands,
with a boy's clear cry.
If I could call the doves
together in the grass—
one of them life
glistening like water,
one of them death
glistening like water,
both warbling deep
inside my secret tree,
blessing the same leaves
with their same song.
If I could call the doves
together in my mouth...

I

THE RULES

The first rule was that he made the rules.
The second: we obeyed them.
The worst rule was that rules changed
unpredictably if he was losing.

There was a rule that split us into teams.
A rule about no starting over.
According to the rules, our mother,
forced to choose, always chose him.

And though the game was nameless,
we could have called it *Abraham and Isaac*.
My brother hauled the wood, the flint, the knife
as our father made a bonfire of his anger.

There was a rule about the first-born son—
the lone, unbroken one that saved me.

MY LOVELY ASSISTANT

After the episode of *That's Incredible!*
in which a whole family of Armenians
in sequined shirts ate fire
and spewed blue, burning plumes, my brother
tied a cottonball to a bent coathanger
and dipped the end in gasoline.

What made us who we are,
one crazy, fearless—one always afraid?
I stood by the ping-pong table
in our mother's only sparkly dress,
playing the role of *Patricia, Lovely Assistant*

because he was bigger than me,
and a master of the headlock,
and threatened, with his breath of snot
and bubble gum and cigarettes,
a vicious wedgy if I didn't.

So I handed him the silver Zippo,
not knowing what future waited for my brother,
still thinking I could save him
who hated being saved—

who took my dare one night to lie
on the yellow stripe of Brown's Bridge Road
and stayed there talking to himself,
pointing to a satellite adrift among the stars,
while I begged him to get up.

Who sat in an upstairs bedroom
giggling at the click of our father's .38.
Who loved the sting of the torch
sizzling his spit-glazed tongue.

So I kept one eye on the door, knowing
from experience how it would end,
how all things turned finally to anger
in that house, where he leaned back, shark-eyed,
and took a swig from the red gas can,
the spitting image of our father in a rage.

He stood between me and that pain.
Knowingly, he raised the magic wand up to his lips.
I sit and wonder what it means—
my brother's sweet face
bursting into flames.

TO FORTUNE

He that hath wife and children
hath given hostages to fortune.
                    —FRANCIS BACON

O my black providence, O my as yet
unimagined pestilence of wind—
of flood, of fire, of whatever it is you choose,
by whose grace or whim we live—

unfork your tongues of phosphorescence
from the frayed wires in my wall; relent
O litany of all that's to be lost
inside the whispering oven;

from your endless work rest long enough,
at least, to listen to my prayer;
and for no reason, as you do all things,
believe me when I swear

O coiled worms of darkness, O bullets
in the oily chambers of forgotten guns,
I have no sleeping wife with golden hair,
no blue, soft moonlit son.

PICTURES OF THE DEAD

How could they know that they no longer are
what, within each little square, they are?

Frozen there like children playing tag, like they'll
wake when we get to where they are.

Some days they look at us like nobody we know.
Like the exquisite paper dolls they are.

And some days with a glance we smell their hair.
Smoke and leaves. That autumn where they are.

What do you want from me? some seem to say,
half-dead already. Now so clearly dead before they are.

And each time we look, the glossy windows darken.
Even the dogs stop wondering where they are.

We stare at ourselves, arm in arm with them.
Children point and ask us who they are.

THE CHIMNEY

Inside the chimney my father built
with stones we hauled from Six Mile Creek,
above the flue, beneath the soot,
is a penny I watched him press into the mortar

before he hefted another slab of shale,
another fractured gypsum brick,
so after the pitched roof falls,
after the shingles and cherry rafters crack

and burn in someone else's fire,
until the chimney stands marooned
in the clearing in the woods, and later falls,
smooth stones sliding down the hill,

when someone, a young man walking to the creek mouth,
stops at the glint from a rock, mica or quartz,
and finds a coin so black and thin
he can barely read the year—

then, my father said, someone will think of him,
long ago pulling the penny from his pocket
and pressing it against the drying chimney,
leaving his long thumbprint swirling.

ELEGY ENDING IN A DREAM

I thought it was like being broken.
It's like being filled with cold sand.

I thought it was fleeting, like passion.
All night in your place the plate shines.

I thought love was the meaning of heaven.
Even heaven turns to shit on my tongue.

I thought *we die* meant like the sun.
All day the sun sinks in the limbs.

I thought a squirrel's nest had blown down.
And found nestled inside it your hands.

BLUE RIDGE BESTIARY

1. Vulture

Business never slows for the air's ubiquitous
morticians, their spiraling so effortless

we might admit its beauty if we didn't know
how eagerly, in those ridiculous black boas,

they wait to begin the endless dissipation
we take as proof: we've been forsaken,

unable to believe our angels of deliverance
rise even to the murky heaven of catfish.

2. Catfish

Greedy face of the zoot-suited villain
in a movie, sharpening his dagger-thin

moustache: sonsabitches I'd wish against
each time the bobber ducked and danced—

who swallowed all my best lures whole
and hissed, as with the crusted needle-nose

I ripped the hook and the hooked heart out
of a thousand, gasping cotton mouths.

3. Cottonmouth

The cure for life, said Socrates, is dying.
The cure for snakebite: slice your skin,

suck poison, then the guidebook says breathe
easily as the viper glides through brittle leaves.

A pit in its face can see your thudding heart.
Its flicked tongue tastes you sweating in the dark.

And even the severed head strikes with venom,
as if death's never dead, just playing possum.

4. Possum

Of all the corpses, none's more easily forgotten
than those bellies strewn beside the road. Rotten

entrails flaking into the treads of tires,
dark shapes hunkered on the lowest wires

as the whole scene flares in that brief brightness
through which we hurtle past each oracle, oblivious

of what it means to see them suffer
and rise from ashes on the wings of vultures.

THE DOE

What does it matter
what I was thinking
when I aimed at a quivering branch
and braced my whole body
for the kick of that Browning .410?

All I could do was watch
the wet-velvet leg of something *alive*
sliding from the spattered white haunches
of the thing that lay dead on the snow.
All I could do was wait

while my father laid a hand on her belly,
unsnapped the strap
of the scabbard that hung from his belt,
then opened her pelt with a jerk
as a steaming blue hose spilled out,

a sopping pouch like a red jellyfish,
and a leathery knot that he worked
out of the ribs in his fist—
lifting his big hands from the carcass
and smearing his cheeks till they shined.

All I could feel was the sticky stripe
burning when he touched my forehead,
his rough fingers making
what I knew, even then, was a sign:
of manhood, of *forgiveness* I thought

until the wet fawn at our feet
shivered and opened its eyes,
until I saw him thumb a gold shell
into his rifle, then slide
the oily bolt home.

IN THE MUSEUM OF YOUR LAST DAY

there is a coat on a coat hook in a hall. Work-gloves
in the pockets, pliers and bent nails.

There is a case of Quaker State for the Ford.
Two cans of spray paint in a crisp brown bag.

A mug on a book by the hi-fi.
A disc that starts on its own: Boccherini.

There is a dent in the soap the shape of your thumb.
A swirl in the glass when it fogs.

And a gray hair that twines
through the tines of a little black comb.

There is a watch laid smooth on a wallet.
And pairs of your shoes everywhere.

A phone no one answers. A note that says *Friday*.
Your voice on the tape talking softly.

TWELVE VIEWS OF MY FATHER

1

Grown so young she has a name, my father's
grandmother Cleavy Rowe settles into
the portrait's ancient rocking-chair,
having never told a living soul
about her boy who died as
she, for the first time,
holds him.

2

Look, seal-slick and laughing,
all lashes, lips, and glowing teeth,
at this clacketing machine unspooling
the angel who became my father.
Six, seven maybe, diving
into a wave that breaks and breaks.

3

O black-lunged colliers of Wylam,
of Pittsburgh, of Wales,
why do you rise from your graves?
Do you not see how your child, my father,
drives a spike
through the blinding white day?

4

Thick as a mangrove
veined with strangler vines,
the forearm
around my neck
tightens as he sings—
as I touch the gold ring
grown like fence wire
through mossed bark.

5

Exactly as dark as whatever
swallowed the room:
breeze of *Maker's Mark,*
of *Captain Black,*

O stiff beard bristles
brush my lips—

6

I don't know which to prefer,
the scald of shame
or absence.
My father in an eyeless rage
or after.

7

We were always seven
at the table:
me and my brother,
my sister, my mother,
my father, and my father, and my father.

8

Among life's joking poker players,
few-calls-makers, and guys
who know a guy who knows a guy,

I always hear my father dickering
the mortician, saying Pop
never paid retail in his life and would rot
in hell before he'd ride
full-price to heaven.

9

How does the boy become a man
lolling on a gurney?

How could the young nurse know
my father, wagging his index and pinky,
just turned a double-play?

                  Seventeen
as he mumbles through the blue mask *Two
down baby. Two away.*

10

Because we are so far away
the zippered strands of DNA
compose themselves like stalks
in a far corn field, or like dots
of newsprint in a photograph:
of me, my father, and his father's face
flickering, in fear, across my son.

11

Behind the photograph, behind the photograph,
behind the downward-creeping pane,
he stares as only a dead man stares
when no one living knows his name.

12

Somewhere behind my eyes
it's snowing in Lilburn.
Always snowing as I ride
his shoulders
and watch the snow
dust every hill
and valley of my father.

THE MUSSEL

I hated my brother more each time
he threw his body off the pier,
headfirst through thick blue air

into the Warrior River. I was six,
too small to swim in the heavy current,
and sat instead on the last wet slat

and watched the bull's-eyes spread and fade
a long dive's distance from my perch,
all sign of him floating on downriver,

leaving me alone to watch
a coal barge passing through the background
like a small town set adrift.

So I waved my arms and pulled a cord
that hung invisibly above my head,
making the captain make his steam horn bellow,

that sound so low I could almost see it
gusting across the water—
until a pale blur flashed like a fin

and broke the surface: a clenched fist
clutching, as I knew it would, as it did each time,
a mussel lifted from the silty bottom

that no one could reach
but the dolphin king, my brother.
And when he rose, waist-deep and dripping

in the muddy shallows by the pier,
I watched him work a fingernail
into the crevice of the shell,

his wrists and knuckles rippling,
his whole slick body trembling until
the mussel's rigid lips ripped open

and a plume of blood arced into the air.
I stood there, staring at what he'd found
beneath the mussel's wet gray tongue:

a yellow river-pearl that slipped from his fingers
as he walked out of the water past me,
up the mossy boat ramp and across the gravel lot,

carrying, like a present to our mother,
his shivering red hand, glistening
and open to the bone.

BAPTISM

So often have I heard it
I can name the poker players at the table,

all dead now but bald Fred Hall
and famous Dan Vitali,

can see their cans of Pabst
sweating rings into the wood,

and smell, in the first room I remember,
the sweet blue smoke of their cigars.

Over the humming fridge, the clacking Kenmore dryer,
I hear their chairs scrape the floor

as they turn to face my father,
standing by the kitchen sink

in his long black robe, arms spread wide,
blessing the basin of rusty county water.

His thumbs hook into my armpits
as he lifts me up, near the glaring bulb, for all to see,

and in the silence after I am touched
the third and final time, before he sets me down,

I can hear him shouting *ghost,*
then the others, whispering *amen.*

II

CHATTAHOOCHEE

Knowest thou the ordinances of heaven?
canst thou set the dominion thereof in the earth?
Canst thou lift up thy voice to the clouds,
that abundance of waters may cover thee?

—JOB 38: 33–34

1

Like a spirit moving through the flower
of moonlight hanging in the water,
through the depth that never warms
where carp and catfish wallow,

I can almost see the bottom of the lake,
the black bass diving,
dividing the darkness
in the feathery tissue of its gills,

as curl after curl rises from my reel and disappears
through a window's tilted frame,
around a tree stump's rotten bowl,
over a scuttled Lincoln

half-buried in the mud.
Below, clear fins fan the water,

and above I whisper to the dark,
asking it to rise

as I wind in a foot,
then give back a yard of the line,
my finger on the filament feeling
the whittled shape of things, the gnarled

remains of another life—
a mussel-crusted fence post,
a mailbox orange with rust,
the limb of a pine where a tire once hung,

turning all afternoon on the breeze.
My rod bends towards breaking,
then straightens as the fish darts free
through the sunken junkyard

that grows by the weight of one lure
from my tacklebox, its silver spoon spinning
as I reel the snapped line back on the spool,
slack as a fallen kite string.

2

The river is no more than a shimmer
of gray and white dots
in September 1949, as Sorghum Crowe
cranks the arm that raises the bucket

through his reflection deep in a well.
The background is blurry,
sun glaring on water,
on what can only be the Chattahoochee

as it once snaked between hills.
The face in the foreground white
as a bare bulb, stubbled and squinting,
half-listening, or not listening at all

to what the photographer says.
Soon he'll sign the deed to the last tract
in the flood plain, giving birth to the future
as he silently scratches his name,

as the absurd churches, jacked onto flatbeds,
shift on their bricks at the edge of the town,
as the gates of the dam begin to close slowly,
and a man starts a vigil over the river,

marking its rise each day
with a nick on the stilts of Brown's Bridge,
his face reflected at the widening edge.
This dead face doesn't mourn, though:

Sorghum Crowe, who picked up
and moved to high ground,
who looked out over the lake,
smooth and opaque

on warm summer evenings,
and lived his last days
for the wet slap of a fish
breaking the water's wide silence.

3

Some tragedies are comic:
a man dies for twenty-three dollars
but would've done it for less.
In coveralls, a ball cap, black whorls of beard,

he crouches like a catcher
to bury his jar under the magnolia.
He stamps on the mound, smoothes it with his shoe.
There is movement, of course,

order to disorder—the brown river rising,
flooding the house, the barn,
the blossoming magnolia. There is the man
wading down the steps of his porch like a Baptist,

cool water filling his pockets with mica
as he dog paddles over the place
where the shimmer should be, the glint
of the pickle jar through the Chattahoochee.

He takes a long breath before going,
then goes. A small act in the story,

one body floating downstream,
becoming a creature of water:

the brown eyes open,
the blue skin spotted with leeches,
the throat filled with pollen and leaves—
floating upstream the day the flood crests.

Only the living need a spirit
for the physics of buoyancy. For us
there's always a message swirling in the eddy,
a voice in the movements of water.

If the drowned man must speak, then—
as his body, stripped bare, floats away—let him say this:
the oldest instinct is to find what you bury,
to come back and dig up your bones.

4

What would have been
a bridge between mountains, spanning the sky,
is a stage for daredevil boys now,
renewing each year the rust patches

on the ledge where they perch in wet cutoffs,
the tan thighs of even the oldest
trembling over the glass-hard surface below,
as the steel grows slowly too hot for standing

and forces each one to choose:
to climb over the guardrail and watch from the road
or step forward into that nothing
high over the girls looking up from the shore,

high over that world underwater,
where each year at least one is lost
in the tangles of barbed wire that hang
just within reach of the deepest swan dive.

At first it's just what you hoped: the body in flight,
making its easy turn in the air.
Then comes the fist-in-the-gut when you know
you're not flying but falling headfirst,

arms windmilling, then clutching to cover the skull
as it shatters into a swarm of white bees.
Only after the eyes adjust
can you see the pale flash of an ankle,

the blur of another boy's fingers
waving back the body's strong will to rise.
Only when the heart tries to open the rib cage
do you know: that to struggle makes it worse,

the barbs cutting your skin, wasting breath,
until the last silver tube slithers from your lips
and rises, unnoticed by those
watching the smooth surface for a sign.

5

With one eye open I see them
rising and banking,
wobbling in the sky
as they must have been doing

since dawn: looking for food,
looking through the black eyes
in their bloody faces,
at the whole valley laid out—

the hills quilled with pines,
the crooked arm of the shore,
the small square dock where I lie,
rising and falling on the water's taut skin.

They glide patiently, certain of their purpose,
knowing as they do what will come—
that what always comes will come this time, too,
as they gather above me, forming

a circle over the dog on the highway,
a circle over the calf in the pasture,
a circle over the possum face-down in the lake.
They know the changed walk of the maimed,

the jaundiced eye of the snake-bit,
the stagger of the newborn because

this is their place: to carry us over the water,
over the trees and smoking chimneys

to their roost at the mouth of the creek,
where even the dead vulture
heaped by the shore is changed
from feathers into feathers

perched on the limbs of the pine—
high over the dock, where the hungry
return to their tree, bringing
the scattered pieces together again.

TO THE MUSE, FROM WAY DOWNTOWN

It's the old surprise of skin on skin
when, ball in hand, I turn

for a jumper from the baseline,
and let the cracked orange Spalding spin,

its stamped black autograph scraped off,
its hide worn hard and thin, though growing

somehow soft again in that moment when I let it go
and listen to the pump's bent needle

rattling inside the bladder (where it broke
and settled years ago, though spit on to prevent this),

each revolution echoing until the high arc ends,
as I watch what started as a bank shot

drop through the bent red rim, with the swish
of all things good, all things unintended:

blind sky-hooks in traffic, tipped-in passes,
and blessed heaves like this one,

that erred so far it mocks perfection, though I'll take it
to my grave, I say, and vow next time I shoot the rock

to let it fly without condition and leave the end
to the sweaty, thundering gods that trail me.

MY FATHER, PLAYING TENNIS

strikes a figure somewhere between
Australopithecus robustus, with its thick skull-crest
and massive, gnashing jaw,

and *Homo habilis,* that big-brow'd,
tool-making, late-Pleistocenian,
wielding his racquet like a fire-charred limb,

eyes flashing, nostrils flaring
as he stalks the little green ball,
so in love with the chase

it must be a vestigial trait,
coded in the deepest, most ancient folds
of his cerebral cortex,

a throwback to days
when the small, furry thing
darting just out of reach meant *dinner,*

when the zeal with which he smashes
easy volleys smack
at the other guy's face meant *survival.*

Raising his sweat-banded forearm,
thick-boned and coated with black hair,
like the silver-back upland *Gorilla gorilla,*

he lofts the ball softly, cocks his arm,
and then kills it: grunting and spitting,
arms flailing wildly as he charges the net,

while in the far court I stand, just like what I am:
a fur-less, immature *Homo Sapiens sapiens*
staring, weak-kneed, at what I came from.

TWO FIGURES

I remember believing the sting
of the scalpel slicing my cheek,
as it moved down through the dark
of your domed belly, was my first memory.

Inside you, I refused to move, the little rope
looped around me, halting your blood
inside my body—three full minutes
your second heart gone silent,

as the stethoscope moved and pressed,
moved and pressed against you until
someone swabbed a stripe of yellow iodine
and motioned for the tools to cut me out.

I remember being on the bottom
of an emerald pool at Daytona Beach,
watching shafts of sunlight spear the water
and hang like pieces of a dusty chandelier.

A dark shape wavered high above me
where I knew you stood,
having risen from your lounge chair
when the pool grew quiet,

having dropped your book to watch
and wait for that moment
when I'd uncurl and rise to meet you,
blue-faced and gasping.

LOOK

I'd like to ask my mother
why I'm here, straddling
one thigh of her bell-bottom jeans,
listening to her whisper *look*
look sweetie in my ear.

But I can't stop staring
at our fat cat Walina,
ancestor of every cat
that ever roamed that house,

as she blinks back at me,
licks between her claws,
then turns again to eating
the clear, vein-laced skin
stretched over the faces
of her babies squirming
in a pulled-out dresser drawer.

I'd like to ask—but this is back
before anything means
anything, when it all just *is*,
and even the squinting kittens
are like a game my mother made up
to pass the drizzly afternoon.

Back in the cold, dark evening
of childhood, where I'm always
alone: watching Walina
close her mouth around the runt—
the sleepy one, the one too weak
to butt its head against her,
that meows and meows
though no sound comes out,
when she drops it outside the drawer.

This is in the oldest room
of the house behind my eyelids,
where the world began:
where a light bulb pops and flickers
over everything, and no one
ever comes to stop the kitten
from dragging its sack of blood
all over the white linoleum.

A VALEDICTION

I watched you snap a rabbit's spine
while stroking it and cooing.

I heard a shot from the hill you climbed
with a gray-faced dog I loved.

And when I winged a sparrow perching
on a sway-backed power line

you laid your thick hand to its skull
and made the shrieking air stand still.

Did you mean that there's no heaven
on earth but dignity? Did you mean

we too will pray some day for mercy?
All I can do is guess now what you

never said but meant. And pretend
somehow you hear this as you rise,

like when I watched the stillness then,
whispering *Wake up. Fly.*

ARS POETICA: HITTING THE CURVE

The only trouble with hitting a curve ball
is that your knees are in love with your skull.

To make them lean *towards* something someone
has flung with clenched teeth at your chin

you have to fake that your front cleat is soaking
in an old milking pail. And believe for an instant

the truth isn't true—that even the Gods, even
Williams and Cobb, fail more often than not.

It helps to know Plato's *is* from *becomes*—
that the field was a *field,* the bat a creaking ash limb.

To know even your withered, pale father was beautiful
once, the bat falling from his shoulders like silk

as you lift your foot from the bucket and wail
like Achilles, without spilling a drop of the milk.

ARS VIDENDI

Let us allow the swan its swanliness,
the beaded eye its glance,
the massive feet their tumorous
and mossy-clawed blackness.

Let us allow all symbols of the mind
life in time: rain and grime,
sickness, luck, contentedness, malign
flies sipping at the oozing wound.

And if we praise a swan-like grace
in the dancer and her airy dance,
let us recollect imagination's palimpsest:
the swan, the swan's eye black with ants.

BRASS KNUCKLES

Something so pleasing in their heft it's easy
to forget how my grandfather
used them in those days
when everybody knew he kept
a hundred rolled and rubberbanded
in the pocket of his mackintosh.

He drove this big delivery truck,
restocking Hersheys and Pall Malls.
And the story always shows
my father in the back,
sorting the endless stacks
and filching Tootsie Rolls.

In the haze of family lore
it's all idyllic, even 1950s
Birmingham: ball fields and church picnics,
tree-lined streets
where he'd park the panel truck.
But somewhere under the patina

of blackened brass, against my jaw,
is the blood of a man
my grandfather beat near death.

Becawse? he chuckled when I was eight,
I didn't like the look
on that ol' nigger's face.

THE REPTILIAN ANCESTRY OF BIRDS

I think of trumpet swans
in the public garden, of feathers,
if you look close at them,

lapped like armor plate,
like snake-skin,
necks curling

into thick white S's
as if about to strike—
though what they do

instead, of course, is glide
all day, huge and innocent,
like snakes forgiven

temptation, given wings
and raised from the dust.
I think of the two of us,

how the same dark eye
is buried in both faces, is watched
and watches from the shore.

How the swan wobbles past
like a paper boat, nodding
as if in greeting *brother*,

while deep in the reeds the other
sheds his bitter skin
and eats it whole.

MASQUE FOR MY FAMILY

1. Eve

For a time we watched in awe, seeing ourselves
in them: how Cain filled the offering with fruit,

how rams followed Abel to the altar.
And for a time my sorrow was a kind of hope.

But time stood still that day
when the Angel called *What hast thou done?*

in the voice that comes to me in dreams.
Knowing already what he'd done,

whose blood Cain called the blood of lambs,
My son, I said, *Let me wash away this stain.*

That's how I remember him: dark eyes reflecting,
for the first time, my endless shame.

2. Adam

In the sweat of my face I was alone
until she, who knew no word for pain,

delivered us from one another.
I gave thanks for what seemed forgiveness,

and taught my sons to make burnt offerings,
and saw all things prosper at their touch.

I was a young, strong man
when the voice of the Angel came.

But when I found the bloody clothes
in a pile between my wife and Cain—

Have mercy, Lord. I lay down in the dust
and begged to be unmade.

3. Abel

In heaven I've tasted the meat of a lamb,
then held the lamb, whole again, in my arms.

I've asked the Angel in whispers, *Take the scythe
out of his hand. Bend the withered corn in which he waits.*

But each time the answer is the same: It was God's will
to fill the world with trees, the trees with snakes.

His will to make me a hoarder of innocence,
a profiteer of my own brother's grief.

God's will to cast my eyes on the water
each morning when Cain tries to wash the mark away

and meets instead my gaze
shimmering in the River of Gihon.

4. Cain

Sign of the lightning strike, sign of the drought
deep in the rings of the pine.

Mark of my passage through time—stretching
from my eye, where the hand of God plunged,

past the cheekbone, to my lip. Sign
to whoever may doubt, that the tiller of earth

and the fugitive of heaven are one.
That whatever I was, I am his keeper now.

Sign of the sign of the sign of *what happened*—
and happens again each dawn

when I wake from the dream of forgiveness,
the kiss burning my cheek unto ash.

THE NIGHT

When I touched your arm and said goodnight
all you could do was moan,
your blind eyes huge and bluish white,
your chest a nest of bones

when I touched your arm and said goodnight
and smoothed the imprint of my thumb
in your withered wrist, too dry and light,
like balsawood or pumice

when I touched your arm and said goodnight
then heard you in the darkness laughing—
your lungs two tongues of flame so bright
I knew I was only dreaming

when I touched your arm and said goodnight
then woke and found you gone—
and found those black unending nights
a hell I'm banished from.

IN SOLITUDE

You who would see the truth of things
now must look within.
To mend the troubles of your times
retreat from them.
In solitude, look to the stars.
—HENRY VAUGHAN

But what when time and solitude
are that which trouble us?
When to the sky we look and find
no sparking flint, no speaking mist?

What good are your cold stars
against my loneliness?
What wish would I ever wish
on them but one: eternity

among the dead revived.
O my lost friends, O bright
beloved eyes watching us
behind the moonlit sky.

THE DANAÏD

Because she killed her bridegroom in the myth,
the girl's damnation always looks
like regret to me—her hell a shame so great

she wilts against the stone, a wave
of hair thrown forward as she weeps.
A thing so beautiful it hurts to think

of Rodin tracing her spine, loveliest
of all the body's curves, in stone
as I lean across the velvet rope

and look into that shadow
where she rests her cheek:
where Camille Claudel, modeling the pose,

once breathed into a pillow, her laughter
muffled by the bedsheets as he worked.
Though when I kneel down close,

picturing your own face, Love,
longing for your light-lashed eyes, half-closed,
the neck dissolves into unchiseled marble,

her face unfinished, unbegun.
As if what seemed to rise out of the rock
is really falling, drowning in the stone.

MY BROTHER, ON LAKE LANIER

Because it is my turn to ski, and because I'm lazy
and don't kill the engine though I know I should
as my brother swims toward the boat,

and because our father's Evinrude is temperamental
and hasn't been tuned in years—my brother, floating
with one hand on the little ladder, fiddling with the rope,

doesn't hear the gearbox slipping out of neutral
or the drive shaft clunking below the water, engaging
the propeller that has drifted to within inches

of his knee—through which the churning blades pass
so easily that all he feels is a thump that he thinks
must be the last rung of the ladder until he hears me

shrieking, and sees a circle the color of motor oil
spreading out around his body, then around
the drifting boat, and then as far as we can see.

THE FLOOD

Two-thirds of earth, and most of us, is water.
Come life, come death's black, fathomless water.

At the mirror I try to picture the soul.
I raise my cupped hands, full of water.

And think of my birth: the scalpel, my mother's
skin parting like a sea of red water.

In the dream of the flood I'm always the one
looking back, turning into a pillar of water.

I drag a stick through my reflection: there lies
another, whose name is written in water.